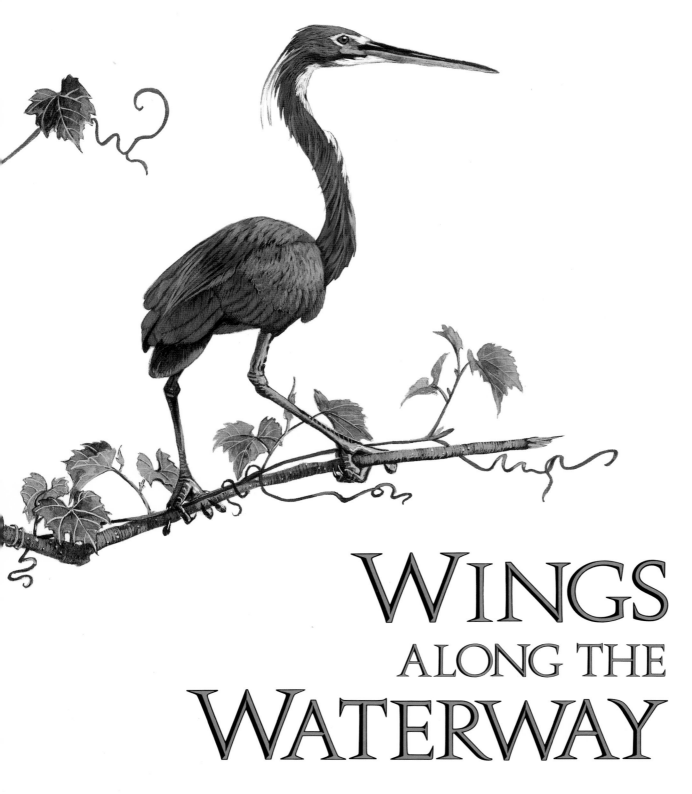

WINGS
ALONG THE
WATERWAY

MARY BARRETT BROWN

   ORCHARD BOOKS · NEW YORK

To Beverly—whose tidbits of information
were always sent with love.

To Karen Klockner and Janet Pascal—my editors—
whose faith, patience, and gentle guidance
made this book come to life.

Acknowledgments

I would like to thank Dr. John Ogden, program manager for wildlife research at
Everglades National Park, and Rosemarie Gnam of the American Museum of Natural History (ornithology department) for reviewing the manuscript for accuracy
and detail.

I would also like to thank Maureen Loughlin (Flamingo District naturalist of Everglades National Park), Ken Christansen of the Treasure Coast Wildlife Hospital,
Wayne Lindsey of the Merritt Island Wildlife Refuge, Nathaniel Reed (former board
member of the National Audubon Society and presently chairman of the Governor's
Commission on the Future of Florida's Environment), and Vireo, at the Academy
of Natural Sciences in Philadelphia, for sharing their time and information.

Finally, I would like to express my deepest gratitude to my husband, Porter, whose
loving support and constructive suggestions were invaluable to me.

ORCHARD BOOKS
387 Park Avenue South · New York, NY 10016

Manufactured in Hong Kong
Printed and bound by Toppan Printing Company, Inc.
Book design by Alice Lee Groton
The text of this book is set in 14 point Bembo.
The illustrations are watercolor reproduced in full color.

10 9 8 7 6 5 4 3 2 1

Library of Congress Cataloging-in-Publication Data
Brown, Mary Barrett. Wings along the waterway / Mary Barrett Brown. p.   cm.
Includes bibliographical references and index. Summary: Discusses the habitat, life
cycle, appearance and habits of twenty-one water birds and examines the risks posed
to them by technological civilization. ISBN 0-531-05981-2.—ISBN 0-531-08581-3
(lib. bdg.) 1. Water birds—Juvenile literature. [1. Water birds. 2. Birds.] I. Title.
QL676.2.B77 1992 598.29'24—dc20 91-18559

Contents

Introduction

The sound of wings breaks the stillness of dawn. One by one and then in flocks, birds fly from their nighttime roosts to the water and its surroundings. Suddenly the landscape is dotted with water birds. All shapes and sizes fill the marshy coves, rushing, almost in silence, to feed. Some earth-colored birds are hard to see as they stalk in the dark shadows of the shoreline. Others, starkly white, stand out sharply. Still others are so vivid they appear to glow in the morning sun.

Although each of these birds is distinct, they all have a common world— the water. It is the water and its environment that is their food source and their shelter—where they mate, nest, and raise their young in the constant pursuit of survival and the preservation of their species.

This book is about some of these birds—about their lives around winding waterways whose paths are fed by marshes, lagoons, and wetlands. Some birds I chose for their beauty, some for their artful camouflage or engaging customs, and some simply because I know them best. All were chosen because of my affection for them.

Great Blue Heron

When a Great Blue Heron stands silently at the edge of the shore, it can be difficult to see. Its blue-gray body and light, streaked neck blend well with the surroundings. Only the stark contrast of its white and black head gives it away. During the breeding season, the heron is at its most elegant. Long, narrow feathers blanket its back, while shorter ones ruffle in the breeze around its neck. On its head two slender black plumes extend from its crest, and its bright yellow eyes become tinged with a delicate red.

Across all North America this stately bird seeks marshes, swamps, rivers, ponds, and other forms of water in which to live. Waterways, especially their swampy edges, teem with life that is the Great Blue Heron's food source. It is a skillful feeder whose long legs, pointed bill, and streamlined body make it easy to hunt for food in deeper water. Although it eats frogs, insects, snakes, and crayfish, fish are its most common food. Sometimes, still as a statue, the heron will wait for prey to swim by. Other times it will stalk noiselessly through the tranquil water. Its attack is swift. With a sudden jerk, the heron's head darts forward. Spearing the fish, it flips it to shore and strikes it until it dies. Then, working the fish into proper position, the heron gulps it down, headfirst.

After feeding, the Great Blue Heron, like other herons and egrets, covers

itself with a soft white powder called powder down. This comes from special feathers that crumble into powder, and is used to condition other plumage. Then, using its bill or the toothlike claw of its middle toe, the heron nibbles or combs the other feathers neatly back into place.

During the breeding season, the male Great Blue Heron must attract a mate. He strikes a pose on a nearby branch, displaying his nuptial plumes. Sometimes, as the female approaches, he can seem strangely unpleasant, stabbing and thrusting his bill at her. Soon, however, they begin their graceful courtship dance. As they stretch their necks and point their bills to the sky, they sway their heads and wail softly. Finally, lifting their feathers, they lower their heads—a signal that they are ready to mate.

High in the bushes or the tops of trees, the Great Blue Heron builds its nest. With sticks and twigs, moss, leaves, and pine needles, it makes a bulky platform. Although they are solitary feeders and will defend their territory fiercely, these herons usually nest in one another's company—or even with other kinds of birds.

After the nest is finished, the female lays three to seven greenish blue eggs. Twenty-eight days later the moist baby Blue Herons chip their way out. Awkward and ugly, they are also very noisy, especially when the parents return to the nest with food. Within ten days the babies are large enough to straggle about the nest. They begin to poke and peck at things—often at one another. This may look like play, but these actions are important to their survival. Since most of their food is found under the water, they must develop the instinct of spearing.

In two or three months the chicks will become fledglings and learn to fly. Like all herons they fly with their heads pulled between their shoulders and their long legs trailing behind. They are beautiful to watch as their graceful strokes carry them over the water and into the trees.

Purple Gallinule

The Purple Gallinule is not a large bird, and in the shadows of the blue-flowered pickerelweed it is difficult to see. In the sunlight, however, its purple feathers glisten like prisms, revealing glossy greens and blues across its lower back. Its yellow and red bill, pale blue forehead, and long yellow-green legs and toes add to its colorful effect. A patch of white shows clearly when it flicks its short, stubby tail.

Although freshwater marshes of the southeastern United States are their most common habitat, Purple Gallinules have been seen as far north as Canada. They also live in other areas, such as the West Indies and South America.

Purple Gallinules weave a shallow nest from the available vegetation, carefully interlacing dead leaves, grasses, reeds, and weeds around living water plants. The decaying leaves and grasses of the nests may help warm their five to ten buff, spotted eggs. For some reason Purple Gallinules sometimes build false nests near the real one. Both parents help sit on the eggs, and in about twenty-one days the black, downy chicks begin to hatch.

Purple Gallinules live in family groups. Some groups are small, with only four members; others are much larger. Except for egg sitting, all the birds share in the work of the parents. Often older offspring help feed and defend the younger baby birds.

When Purple Gallinules wander among the lily pads, they spread out their extremely long toes. This distributes their weight so they can walk upon the floating pads with ease. Although they will eat frogs, snails, water insects, and seeds, a grub that lives in the stems of water lilies forms a special part of their diet. Deftly using their feet to lift up the pads, they pry out the grub with their bills.

Although Purple Gallinules step with grace and ease on the ground, they are rather ungainly when they fly. With flapping wings and dangling legs, they fly for only short distances close to the water's edge. Sometimes instead of flying, they swim across the water, bobbing their heads in cootlike fashion until they reach the other side.

❧ Great Egret ☙
(often called Common Egret)

Great Egrets are also called Common Egrets, for they are among the most widespread type of heron. They range through most of North, Central, and South America, as well as Europe, and are also quite common throughout Africa, Asia, and Australia.

These sleek and graceful birds live in wetland habitats of every kind. They can be found in either saltwater or freshwater surroundings, especially in swamps, seashores, and tidal marshes. Although they fly in large numbers to their feeding grounds and can sometimes be seen by the hundreds in a quiet pond, when food is not plentiful they will also feed alone. As Egrets slip through the water in search of food, their black legs seem to disappear into the surroundings. Some people believe this is a natural way of making their prey believe they aren't a threat.

During the breeding season, long, delicate plumes called aigrettes trail down the Great Egrets' slender white backs, and a tint of green frames their yellow eyes. Their courtship ritual is a dazzling spectacle. In white frenzy two male rivals leap and spar, striking at each other as they compete for the female. Once the fight is over, the victor parades before the female—stretching, strutting, and flaunting his plumes while uttering soft, low, crooning sounds.

After the birds are paired, they begin to build their nest. Occasionally, Great Egrets will nest in bushes or reeds just above the water. More often they are found high in the branches of mangrove, willow, or cypress trees, usually in the company of pelicans, wood storks, ibises, cormorants, and other heron species.

When the nest of twigs has been built and three or four pale aqua eggs have been laid, the parents tend to the quiet task of sitting. But the calm does

not last long. Twenty-four days later the baby egrets chip their way out of the eggshells. Constantly hungry, the babies keep their parents busy feeding them several times a day. Great Egrets may fly as much as five or ten miles to find food for their young. When their parents approach with something to eat, the chicks stretch their necks and squawk a rasping *kek-kek-kek-kek-kek*.

At first the parents put food directly into the noisy nestlings' mouths. Later the parents place it in the nest for them to feed themselves. Their diet is

varied. It consists mostly of fish, frogs, and crayfish, although they will also eat grasshoppers, moths, dragonflies, aquatic insects, and even seeds and small fruits.

Around the beginning of the twentieth century, hunters killed Great Egrets and sold their plumes to decorate hats for ladies. Their feathers were worth nearly double their weight in gold. Today conservation laws protect the Great Egrets, and, for now, they do not face extinction. As development encroaches upon the Egret's wetland habitat, however, its survival is threatened.

 American Coot

Coots are busy, noisy, and aggressive little birds who live in both freshwater and saltwater habitats. They are commonly seen in many parts of the world. In North America they have various names: Marsh Hen, Water Chicken, Mud Duck, and Splatterer, to mention a few.

Coots look something like plump little pigeons or ducks. They are excellent swimmers and divers, but instead of webbed feet like those of many swimming birds, they have lobed feet. Lobes are scaly folds that run down each side of their toes and help them to swim skillfully by acting like paddles.

Coots cannot jump into flight as many birds do. Instead, they must dash across the water, flapping and splashing and beating their wings until, finally, they lift clumsily into the air. When a large flock of Coots takes off together, it is quite a sight!

When they swim about, feeding on tender vegetation, Coots pump their heads and utter funny little clucking sounds. Their diet is varied. Sometimes they eat snails and worms or feed on the mossy green algae that settles along the shoreline. Other times they may dive as far as twenty-five feet to gather the leaves, seeds, and roots of aquatic plants. They are comical to see when they bob back up, tail first.

Coots are rather dull-looking birds except for their special markings. Their bodies are slate gray, with a splash of white hidden under their short, stocky tails. Their beak and legs are creamy white, and they have a hard ivory platelike shield that runs from their beak up onto their forehead. Their eyes are a ruby red that stands out like jewels against the dark color of their heads.

Coots can be quite belligerent at breeding time. Fights frequently occur, both for territory and for mates. Slashing and splashing and flapping their wings, Coots will attack any intruders. When ready to breed, the male swims in front of a potential mate, places his head on the water, and lifts his wings. As he passes back and forth, he raises his tiny tail, spreading it as wide as he can. When she gives a similar display, he flicks his tail and, as if signaling her to follow, slowly swims away.

Their floating nests built of plants and grasses are solidly attached to reeds or cattails so they won't drift away. Both parents help keep the eight to twelve pinkish buff, speckled eggs warm. It takes about twenty-three days for the chicks to hatch. Although they are colorful, with bright red foreheads and red and black bills, they are rather ugly.

As soon as they have hatched and are dry, baby Coots begin to swim. Within a few hours they are diving as well, and before long they are deftly following their parents around the shoreline in search of food.

Yellow-Crowned Night Heron

High in the branches, there is a soft cry. It is the *whoop* of the Yellow-Crowned Night Heron. Head held high, he stretches tall. Suddenly, bending his legs and lifting his feathers, he whoops again with a low, graceful bow.

Yellow-Crowned Night Herons are found in the central and eastern United States, the West Indies, and Central and South America. It is not always easy to see an adult. Their gray-streaked bodies and black and yellowish heads blend well with the dark shadows of the swamps. Only the brilliance of their red eyes and orange legs reveals them to us. The younger birds are also difficult to see. They are dull in color, and their brown feathers outlined in white hide them well in the bushes.

Stepping across a thicket of limbs, the male Yellow-Crowned Night Heron snaps a twig and brings it back to his mate. She raises her feathers in display. Then, while she takes the twig and places it in the new nest, he goes off to gather more.

Both parents help incubate the three to five pale blue-green eggs until, in about twenty-five days, the little chicks are hatched. Covered with a fuzzy gray down, they have dark yellow eyes that are open the moment they have pipped from their eggs. Their pinfeathers appear ten days later, but it will still be nearly two months before they grow the brown and white juvenile feathers needed to fly.

Yellow-Crowned Night Herons have many calls—perhaps as many as twenty. When courting, they use a low whooping sound, and they also make *yups* and *woks* and screeching *squawks,* especially when they are disturbed.

A solitary feeder, the Yellow-Crowned Night Heron quietly stalks around swamps, bogs, slow-moving rivers, and ponds where crayfish and crustaceans abound.

Much of the time these birds feed at night when the other birds have left and the crayfish and crabs are more active. They will at times, however, search for food during daylight if the tide is low or ebbing.

Watching a heron hunt for food can be hypnotic. Eyeing its prey, the heron pauses. Then, inch by inch, it moves. With agonizing slowness it pulls up one foot and places it in front of the other. The heron waits, its eyes never leaving its mark. So slow is the bird that an hour can pass and only a few steps will have been taken. Moving closer to its prey, the heron gradually lowers its neck and its body begins to sway. Suddenly, in one swift darting plunge the Yellow-Crowned Night Heron feeds.

Limpkin

When the Limpkin calls, its sorrowful cry pierces the dark, somber sky. To a listener it may seem to be lamenting its own dwindling kind.

Limpkins live near the freshwater swamps and sluggish rivers of southeast Georgia and the peninsula of Florida. They also range as far south as the West Indies and South America. Once hunted for their flavorful meat, they are now protected by law, but they still face the danger of destruction. Drainage of the wetlands and natural dry spells have drastically reduced their food source.

Although Limpkins eat mollusks, insects, frogs, and lizards, it is the apple snail of the Everglades they seek out most. Stepping and probing in the shallow water, a Limpkin will suddenly snatch a snail from the mud. Flying awkwardly to the shoreline, it places the snail upside down on an old stump. Then, using its long, perfectly designed bill, the Limpkin pries out the snail with a few swift tugs, leaving the shell unbroken. One can always tell where a Limpkin has eaten by the piles of empty shells resting along the shoreline or near a fallen log.

Limpkins blend well with the earthen color of their surroundings. Only white streaks and splotchy patches break up the monotonous tones of their dark brown feathers. While the Limpkin gets its name from the way it seems to limp about, this is really only a mannerism. These birds can be stealthy and slip through the tall, reedy grasses like fleeting shadows. They are fine swimmers and waders, and their long toes help them tread lightly on the muck and mire along the banks.

Just above the waterline, the Limpkin builds its nest of dried leaves and reeds woven into the surrounding living grasses. In spring, when the baby Limpkins hatch, they are covered with dark, thick, brownish down, with lighter patches on their throats and bellies. As the little birds fledge, they quickly learn, like their parents, to swim and to slip silently in and out of the reeds.

Anhinga-Anhinga

The name Anhinga-Anhinga, or simply Anhinga, dates back to the Indians of the Amazon jungles. It means "water turkey," because this bird resembles a turkey when it flies. Some people also call the Anhinga Snake Bird, because it can sink into the water until only its head and long, curved neck are seen.

Awkward on land, Anhingas move clumsily among the branches of swampland trees. But in the water or flying high, they are graceful, especially when they soar in the heat of the day, joining vultures and ospreys drifting in wide, slow circles.

Anhingas are masterful swimmers who probe beneath the surface of the water for their food. When they spot a fish, their heads dart forward, and they spear it. Rising to the surface, they toss the fish into the air and then swallow it headfirst.

Like their relatives the cormorants, Anhingas have feathers that are not waterproof. After swimming or eating, they perch on banks or low-lying limbs to dry their water-soaked wings. With their dusky olive and yellow webbed feet clinging to the branches, these dark birds with speckled wings appear almost prehistoric as they glisten in the noonday sun.

Anhingas often nest in small colonies with herons and egrets, or just other Anhingas. To attract a female, the male builds a nest of twigs and lines it with freshly picked leaves and moss. Standing tall, he raises his neck and tail feathers while bending his neck into snakelike curves. At times he will stretch his wings and display the silvery design. During this time of courtship, the skin around his eyes turns to a vivid aqua green (as does the female's). When a buffy-necked female responds to his dance, the two of them touch—crossing their necks, rubbing their bills, and nibbling at each other.

After the four or five pale blue eggs are laid, the male and female Anhingas take turns warming them. In a few weeks small, wet babies pip their way into the world. For a while they are helpless—able only to open their wide little mouths for food. But they grow, becoming buff colored and strong. Soon they will fledge, and the time will come for them to fly.

Osprey

Water sprays. An Osprey rises, straining with the large fish held tightly in its talons. Worldwide, wherever there is a bay or a river, seacoast or lake, Ospreys will probably be found.

These mighty birds hover high above the water until they spy a fish. Suddenly, with legs thrust forward and wings held high, they plunge. Using their well-adapted feet, they rotate their outer toes to the back to grasp the fish securely. Rough pads under their toes help strengthen their unyielding grip.

Until recently, a pesticide called DDT threatened the Osprey's existence. When DDT ran into the water, the fish that the Ospreys ate became poisonous. This made the shells of their eggs too thin to hold the chicks inside, and their population dwindled. In 1972 DDT was banned. Now the Osprey is rapidly returning.

Easy to find, their huge, bulky nests are built of sticks and moss or other debris. A dead or dying tree is a likely site, but Ospreys will also nest on channel markers, poles, rooftops, chimneys, rocks, or the ground—whatever is available. Even though a nest may need to be fixed up, Ospreys usually return to the same one year after year.

Depending on where they live, Ospreys may lay their three pale pinkish brown spotted eggs anytime from December until June. The female usually tends the eggs while the male brings food.

About five weeks later the baby chicks hatch. For two months they are under their parents' protective care. As summer progresses, the fledglings begin to fly. Awkward at first, they do not venture far from the nest. But soon they are nearly grown and have mastered flight, and they wing their way out into the world.

American Bittern

Because it points its bill skyward when hiding, the Bittern is sometimes called Sun Gazer. The booming, pumping sound of its voice has also earned it such nicknames as Thunder Pump and Stake Driver.

As ice and cold begin to sweep across their habitats, northern Bitterns fly to the warmer climate of the Gulf Coast states. Southern Bitterns do not need to migrate. These birds range all over the United States and Canada, but they are so secretive that it is difficult to find them.

Bitterns have a special mannerism when alarmed or threatened: they freeze, with their necks stretched out and their bills pointed to the heavens. If an alligator or other predator passes menacingly close by, the Bittern does not move. It watches, motionless. Its body, heavily streaked with brown and white, is well hidden in the haven of reeds and cattail stalks.

Bitterns feed around marshes, ponds, and slow-moving rivers. They do not usually perch on branches but, instead, wait at the water's edge. When a frog, insect, fish, or small snake comes by, the Bittern slowly lengthens its neck, then swiftly jabs the prey with its bill.

Unlike most herons, Bitterns do not nest in colonies. The male usually chooses the nest site, while the female builds the nest. She stays very busy, for not only does she build the nest, she also incubates the four or five eggs and then feeds the chicks after they have hatched. A Bittern's nest is very difficult to find. Whether it is built just above the water or on the ground, it is well hidden in the dense, protective cover of the shore. Only the paths that lead to the nest might give it away.

Buff-colored down covers the baby Bitterns when they hatch. Although it will be awhile before they have the streaked camouflage underbodies of their parents, they already mimic the freezing technique, even though they look awfully silly when they do.

Little Blue Heron

It is a slender bird, the Little Blue, with lovely slate and purple plumage. Its yellow eyes and black-tipped bill contrast strikingly with the green foliage edging the shore. The Little Blue tends to stay alone in secluded spots. It does, however, mingle with tricolored herons and, at times, white ibises. It is often seen wading in the inland wetlands and freshwater rivers and lagoons, along the Atlantic coast and down to the West Indies and parts of South America.

Like most herons, the Little Blue has a varied diet of fish, insects, frogs, tadpoles, and other aquatic animals. In Louisiana, where it eats the crayfish that live along the rice levees, people have nicknamed it the Levee Walker.

As the Little Blue Heron walks slowly through the water, searching for prey, it will often pause and peer attentively into a pool. When it does this, its shadow helps reduce the glare. Sometimes, to excite the fish, the Little Blue will suddenly run and hop, quickly flicking its wings and stirring the muddy water with its fast-moving spindly feet. It has also been known to follow white ibises and feed on the prey that they have startled. It may catch twice as many fish this way as it would otherwise.

Little Blues roost, or sleep, together, as do many water birds. They may do this for warmth, or perhaps for safety from predators. Some people think the younger birds stay close to the older ones in order to follow them to good feeding grounds.

The Little Blue Heron makes many expressive sounds. Sometimes, just as it lands, it will set its wings, stretch its neck, and utter a series of croaking calls. This may be a kind of greeting. When frightened or alarmed, the Little Blue may raise its plumes and sound loud, raucous croaks. If disturbed by another bird, it may also lunge foward, lifting its wings while jabbing and snapping its bill at the offender.

In the dense growth of willows, cypress, or mangrove trees, colonies of Little Blues grunt and mutter while building their small, frail nests of twigs. The male gathers a twig and holds it out to the female, who weaves it into the flimsy platform. Sometimes they pause and nibble at each other's feathers.

Taking turns, the Little Blues warm the four or five eggs. If something should frighten the sitting parent, it will cry out with loud, grating croaks. Twenty-four days later, one by one, the chicks begin to hatch.

One of the most unusual features of the Little Blue Heron is the color of its young. Instead of having the dark, rich feathers of the adults, these juvenile herons are pure white. For this reason they are easily confused with Snowy Egrets, although their yellow-green legs and bluish bills do distinguish them. As Little Blue Herons grow into adulthood, their white plumage becomes speckled and splotched with new blue feathers. During their second summer, they finally molt into the splendid colors of the full-grown bird.

~ Snowy Egret ~

During the breeding season, the Snowy Egret grows slender filmy plumes. As a soft breeze blows, it suddenly displays, and its feathers lift up in hundreds of long, lacy wisps. It is a graceful figure of white, with a black bill and astonishingly bright golden feet.

In the past this heron was endangered. Years ago, plume hunters killed Snowy Egrets by the thousands and sold their fibrous plumes to decorate women's apparel. Today they are protected and they now range and breed along the coasts and large, inland wetlands of North and South America and the West Indies.

When feeding, the Snowy Egret has many techniques. It may wade slowly in the shallows, peering into the cool water, or suddenly scamper about, hopping here and there, probing and poking, stirring up the mud with its yellow feet. Sometimes it will vibrate the water with its bill to attract nearby fish or, like the little blues, will follow ibises and feed on the fishes that have been stirred up.

Although they are fiercely protective of their territory, Snowy Egrets will nest together in colonies, often with other species of herons. The colonies are noisy places, with hundreds of herons, egrets, and their nestlings all calling at once. Although Snowy Egrets will build on the ground, they generally nest in dense bushes or trees, at a height of eight to ten feet.

When spring courting begins, males often group together, displaying their breeding plumes. Sometimes they point their bills to the sky and bob their heads up and down, uttering an *awa-awa-waa* cry. Sometimes they circle in the air, then suddenly tumble over and over toward the ground.

A male Snowy Egret brings sticks, twigs, and bits of reeds that the female uses to build the nest, making it large enough to hold four or five pale blue-green eggs.

Three weeks later the baby birds hatch. After only a few days these prickly-looking puffs of white are ready to exercise their legs and wings. While the parents watch, the chicks circle around the stalky nest, hopping and jumping and flapping about. This can be dangerous, however, for if a chick falls, it may become food for a passing alligator, raccoon, or turtle.

When the chicks begin to wander about the branches, instead of feeding them in the nest the parents wait on nearby limbs with food. Each day the chicks gain strength. Feathers take the place of their puffy down, and about thirty days from the time they have hatched they are ready to fly.

Black Skimmer

When dusk comes and the tide is ebbing, small fishes and crustaceans leave the exposed shelter of nooks and coves and gather near the surface of deeper water. Now is the time that the Black Skimmers feed. With mouths open wide, they fly low over the water, slicing their long lower bills through it, ready to scoop up their prey.

These slender birds look like black-and-white photographs highlighted with touches of red. No other bird has a bill quite like the Skimmer's, with

the lower half longer than the upper half. When it touches a passing fish, the upper bill instantly snaps shut. With a jerking head, the Skimmer lifts its bill and, without slowing its flight, swallows the fish and continues on its hunt. The Skimmer's eyes are also unusual. Catlike and dark, the pupils are vertical and can become slits in an instant for protection from the glare of the sand and sun.

Black Skimmers can often be seen standing statuelike, facing the wind on sandy bars or islets. If disturbed, however, the flock will suddenly rise and move in perfect unison to a nearby bar or beach. Some people believe they may have a leader who signals the movement.

Skimmers' nests are simple, shallow dishes that the females scoop out of the sand. They nest in large colonies of up to several hundred pairs, often with sea gulls and terns. Their three to five speckled, cream-colored eggs blend well with the sandy surroundings, as do the little Skimmer chicks when they hatch.

At first the young stay close to home while the parents bring them meals. Sometimes the young will try to hide by scratching into the hollow and kicking sand over themselves. Soon, however, when the little ones begin to grow up and turn brown, they start to wander around their sand and water world. Only when they have fledged and are nearly ready to fly and catch their own food will their lower bills begin to grow faster and longer than their upper ones.

Green-Backed Heron
(or Little Green Heron)

A dark-colored bird, the Green-Backed Heron is a shiny, deep slate green, with rich chestnut coloring on its sides, and a small patch of white on its throat. During the breeding season, its yellow eyes and dusky legs turn a bright red-orange, and its crown feathers become long, shaggy, and fanlike.

The Green-Backed Heron can make a terrible racket. From a piercing *skow* to a screeching *skeow,* its voice echoes across the water. When disturbed, it may call *skuk-skuk-skuk-skuk.* Sometimes, when not calling loudly, the Green-Backed Heron may make quiet clucking and clacking sounds—especially the male when courting.

Except for the mating season, Green-Backed Herons most often stay alone—apart even from their own kind. Because they are small, they usually feed around the edges of ponds, rivers, and marshy woodlands in both salt and fresh water. They are common around much of the United States, northern South America, and the West Indies. Fish are their main food source, but they also eat prawns, crabs, small snakes, grasshoppers, and dragonflies. Usually they crouch on a low limb or broken branch just above the water. When they see the prey, they stretch their necks and, in a split second, seize it. In some areas, such as Japan, Green-Backed Herons have been seen scattering berries and insects over the water as bait to lure the fish.

When a Green-Backed Heron rapidly raises and spreads its crest feathers while flicking its short stubby tail, it is probably performing a courtship display. It also hops about from one foot to the other, swaying and dancing in circles while uttering a soft *oooo* call.

In an instant Green-Backed Herons can change their pose so they look almost like a different bird. They may hunch until they almost disappear in the tangles of the dark, swampy shoreline. If menaced, they may raise their crests while clicking their tails, stretch their necks, or perhaps simply freeze in place. Sometimes, as if trying to peer over a towering wall, Green-Backed Herons will stretch their necks higher and higher until they look almost like tall, slender, feathery tubes.

Green-Backed Herons fly in several ways. After taking off, they may lengthen their necks and fly in large, wide circles. Then, for no apparent reason, they return to their starting point. They may also fly with dangling legs and a crooked neck while making soft flapping sounds with their wings.

White Ibis

Like many of the long-legged birds of the marshes and swamps, the Ibis has narrow, slender toes that help it walk on the silt and mud without sinking down. Its long, bright red, down-curved bill is well suited to probing in holes and crevices in the mud for food such as crayfish and crabs. These birds are valuable to their water environment. Crayfish consume vast numbers of fish, so the Ibis, by eating crayfish, helps maintain the delicate natural balance.

Proper water levels and plenty of food are vital to the White Ibis's survival. If the water tables vary dramatically, causing the fish and crayfish to die or disperse, the number of Ibises will dwindle. They may not lay eggs, or they may move elsewhere in search of food. In some areas where there have been droughts, White Ibises have been seen feeding, not by the water, but around landfills and garbage piles.

When they fly in formation to their roosts at the end of the day, White Ibises seem to fill the sky. They nest in huge colonies, usually in the dense brush of mangrove trees or in large freshwater marshes around the southern and eastern United States coastal areas—often in the company of herons, egrets, anhingas, and other birds. Their nests of twigs and branches are quite bulky and are generally placed on low-lying limbs that extend out over the water. Sometimes they line their nests with leaves or moss to cushion the eggs. Just as often, however, the eggs will be laid on the bare, hard, knobby sticks and twigs.

In only three weeks the babies hatch. At first unattractive, with full grayish down, the nestlings soon molt into brown and white fledglings. It takes about two years before their feathers become as white and as brilliant as their parents'.

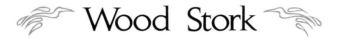 Wood Stork

Soaring on warm air currents, Wood Storks drift for miles to their feeding grounds. To see so many of these large birds at one time makes it difficult to believe they are endangered and may someday become extinct.

Wood Storks are voracious eaters: an adult can eat several pounds of fish a day. Because they feed by feeling with their immense bills, they must live in areas where fish and other aquatic life are abundant. As cities spread out and wetlands are drained, the fish population is reduced. Without enough food to eat, the Wood Storks will die too. Like all water birds, Wood Storks are intimately connected to their environment. The balance and harmony between the two must be maintained in order for them to survive.

The Wood Stork is the only stork found in the United States. It lives primarily in Florida and eastern Georgia, although it is beginning to migrate into South Carolina in a constant search for food. Some Wood Storks that live in Mexico range into southern California, Texas, and parts of Louisiana, but they do not mix with their eastern relatives.

They are large birds, about three and a half feet tall, with a wingspan of over five feet. It is hard to say whether they are beautiful or awesomely ugly.

Their glistening white bodies against the black tips of their flight feathers create a striking contrast of color. From their necks up, however, they are odd-looking creatures, craggy and bald, with scaly skin and huge, thick, roughened beaks. Because of their strange appearance they have been nicknamed Ironhead, Flinthead, and Preacher. They also have been called Wood Ibises, but actually they are not related to the ibis.

Wood Storks need several months to court, mate, nest, hatch, and care for their young. This is a crucial time, for they need a long period of calm. Even without dry spells in winter or the drainage of their habitat, they may be threatened. If heavy summer rains arrive, the waterway and its wetlands will flood and scatter the Wood Stork's concentration of food.

To build their nests, Wood Storks search for swamps where cypress or mangrove trees grow. They build close together high in the trees—as high as one hundred feet. If the Wood Stork colony has plenty of food, about three or four creamy white eggs are laid in the nest. If food is scarce, they will lay fewer eggs.

When the young Wood Storks hatch, they are like noisy miniature replicas of their parents, only covered with dense, woolly down. They are helpless little creatures and must spend seven weeks in the nest before they are ready to roam around their water surroundings.

Roseate Spoonbill

Like so many water birds, Roseate Spoonbills were once hunted for their beautiful plumes. Sanctuaries and laws protect them now, but although their population is increasing, they are not yet abundant, and they are still threatened by the human development of their natural habitat.

As they wade slowly in the shallow water of southern coastal swamps and bays, they swing their massive, spoonlike bills back and forth in search of food. The nerve endings inside their mouths are so sensitive that, as soon as their bills touch a fish or crustacean, their mouths snap shut and the prey is caught.

The lovely pink color of the Roseate Spoonbills comes from their diet of fish and crustaceans. There is a substance in their food called carotene. Although the process is not fully understood, carotene, when eaten, causes changes in their system that produce their color.

These are handsome yet homely creatures. Their naked heads are craggy and small, and their long bills appear to be flattened, but their pink and white colors balance the effect of their grotesque faces.

Their bulky nests, which they may build in the branches of a red mangrove tree, hold three large, buff, speckled eggs. When the baby Spoonbills straggle from their shells, they are defenseless and ugly, bearing little resemblance to their striking parents. Before long, however, they gain strength and begin to climb among the branches. Their blunt bills begin to widen, and their sparse pinkish down becomes soft, woolly, and thick.

In the dusky glow of twilight, Roseate Spoonbills can be seen for miles as they stream across the sky. Looking like puffs of cotton candy, they fly in procession to the safety of their nighttime roosts.

Brown Pelican

Pelicans have hardly changed in their millions of years on earth. They have been honored, used as symbols, revered—and nearly destroyed.

Unlike other kinds of pelicans, who often live in large inland lakes and marshes, the Brown Pelican is strictly a bird of seacoasts and coastal rivers. Also unusual is the Brown Pelican's method of feeding, for it is the only one of the world's several species of pelicans that dives from the air for its food.

A few years ago, the pesticide DDT began to poison the fish that Brown Pelicans eat. This caused their eggshells to become too thin and break before the babies were ready to hatch. Soon the Pelicans faced extinction. Now that DDT is banned, the pelican population is returning.

Brown Pelicans are marvelous technicians of flight. Whether sailing or soaring, taking off or landing, they use the currents of air to make their flying easier. When they seem to be "following the leader," they are not really playing a game. They are simply taking advantage of the air currents created by the bird ahead. Sometimes Brown Pelicans can be seen flying just above the surface of the water. By flying low, they press down the air beneath their bodies, creating a sort of pillow on which to glide.

As the warm air rises in the late heat of the day, a parade of Brown Pelicans flies lazily above the gentle swells of the bay. Following the leader, they sail and glide, breaking the rhythm from time to time with slow-motion flaps of their wings. Suddenly, tilting over, they dive. With their necks tucked in and their wings half-closed, they plummet toward the water. At the last moment their necks stretch out as they dive deep into a school of fish. In an instant their bills open up, and their flexible pouches expand into massive containers. They scoop up the fish and gallons of water, bob to the surface, drain off the water, and swallow their plentiful catch.

Brown Pelicans have a vivid, if silent, courtship dance. Standing before

the female, the male rotates his head over and over in sweeping figure-eight motions. Later, as the female rests on the ground, he circles around her, raising his wings and tilting his head to his back.

Sometimes Brown Pelicans nest in trees, sometimes on the ground. In the trees their nests are built mainly of sticks and branches, with grasses and reeds for a cushion. On the ground they may be only shallow scoops or mounds of soil lined with bits of debris.

Newly hatched Brown Pelicans are perhaps the ugliest of all baby birds. At first they are pink and naked. About twenty-four hours later, their bodies take on a blackish purple tone. This is a dangerous time for them. The parents must stay close by, for the nestlings must not get overheated or chilled and are completely dependent on their parents' care.

For the first ten days the parents feed the chicks by regurgitating food or placing it directly in the nest. After ten days or so, the nestlings are strong enough to reach into the parent's pouch and feed by themselves.

Raucous and noisy when they are young, Brown Pelicans, like other pelican species, begin to lose their voices as they grow older. After a while they make hardly any sound at all—a stunning contrast to their frenzied chorus as chicks.

 Common Tern

Terns face many dangers. Owls and other predators often kill them. Little tern chicks may be fatally stabbed when they trespass into another bird's territory, or storms and high tides may flood the ternery and sweep away thousands of eggs and young. Diseases may descend upon the colony, killing the newly hatched birds. Terns are survivors, however, and when the seasons are good, they respond and recover quickly.

Common Terns feed by diving for fish that swim near the surface of the water. Hovering above, they will suddenly plunge when they spot a school of fish swimming beneath them.

Sandy sites such as an islet or a beach are ideal places for Common Terns to nest. Thousands of other terns and sea gulls may have already arrived, but even in the most crowded quarters there always seems to be enough room.

When courting, the male struts about with his neck stretched out, his head held high, and tail raised and fanned. An equally important part of the courtship ritual is the fish he gives to the female. As they select their nest site, the male continues to bring fish to his mate.

Building the nest is a simple affair. Lying down, the Tern rotates in circles while scooping out sand with its feet. Once in a while the nest will be lined with shells and seaweed or perhaps some sticks or reeds, but most often it is left bare.

After about twenty-five days the two or three speckled eggs begin to hatch, and the baby terns emerge as little brown fluffs. For the first day or two they remain in the nest while their parents shield them from the weather and possible intruders. But before long the chicks begin to roam around on their own.

At the beginning of the twentieth century, Common Terns were nearly annihilated by plume hunters. Later they were given legal protection, and now Common Terns can be found worldwide, wherever the fishing is good and the water abundant.

Tricolored Heron
(once called Louisiana Heron)

Because of this bird's dainty, delicate manner, Audubon, the great scholar of birds, nicknamed the Tricolored Heron Lady of the Waters. It is surely one of the most stunning of all herons. Although its supple neck and long, slender bill give it a sleek appearance, it is the pure white of its underside against its slate and cinnamon back that makes this bird so elegant.

The Tricolored Heron is found in the eastern and southern coastal United States, northern South America, and the West Indies. Wading along marshy shorelines, this heron sometimes stretches out one leg to muddy the water and stir up a flush of fish. More often it prances about with wings outstretched, snatching up minnows, frogs, crayfish, and other aquatic animals. Possibly its color helps it feed, since its white underbody may offset its shadow, thus deceiving the fish.

In early spring Tricolored Herons grow graceful, long, white head feathers that signal the beginning of their time of courtship. Bowing low to the female, the male steps out on a lowlying limb. Every now and then, he will raise his plumes and strike a handsome pose. After a while he slowly sidles back to her. Finally touching each other, they rub each other's heads, intertwine their necks, and mate.

In the dark junglelike growth of mangrove and willow clumps, Tricolored

Herons build their nests. They often form nesting colonies with many other herons and egrets. Taking sticks and branches from nearby trees, the male brings them to his mate. While he raises his feathers and struts about, she responds by raising her feathers too. Then, taking the stick he has brought to her, she weaves it into place.

The parents take turns warming the three or four pale greenish blue eggs. About three weeks later the baby birds begin to hatch. Because the eggs are not all laid at the same time, it may take several days for them to be pipped. The nestlings are odd-looking creatures, with bulging eyes and short spikelike feathers sticking up from their heads. Still, the soft brown down across their backs and the white of their bellies give a hint of their future beauty.

Pied-Billed Grebe
and
Common Loon

Dive Dapper is an apt nickname for the Pied-Billed Grebe, which swims and dives so well underwater. This little bird, like other grebes, acts so much like a Loon that people once thought they were related. Both Grebes and Loons feed by diving from the surface and swimming underwater, and both eat the same food—fish in particular. Both can deflate the air in their bodies in order to sink gently under the water. To help them swim and dive underwater, the legs of Grebes and Loons are built far back on their bodies; however, this makes walking on land awkward; and to fly, Grebes and Loons must dash across the water for quite a long way before they become airborne.

Grebes' nests are built on floating mats of reeds, rushes, and bits of mud attached to grasses growing in the shallow shores. Loons' nests, although similar, are usually built in sheltered coves, not actually in, but near the water.

The toes of the Pied-Billed Grebe are lobed, whereas the Loon's are webbed; nevertheless, both are beautifully designed for swimming. Both Grebe and Loon chicks learn quickly to swim and dive. The chicks will often climb onto a parent's back and ride there. In fact, the chicks are so secure in the water that their parents can safely dive with them aboard.

Although they are similar in many ways, Pied-Billed Grebes and Common Loons do have some differences. The Grebe is about twelve to fifteen inches long, only half the size of a Loon. Loons usually mate on land, while Grebes mate on their nests. Loons lay two or three spotted eggs. Grebes lay seven or eight unspotted eggs. Grebes eat their own feathers, perhaps because their gizzards cannot crush the bones in their food, and their feathers act as soft padding until the bones dissolve. Loons do not need to do this.

Unlike the Loon, whose dazzling black and white pattern clearly identifies it on northern lakes in the summer, the Pied-Billed Grebe is a somewhat drab little bird. Its only clear summer marking is the black band that circles its white chickenlike bill. For some reason this band disappears in winter. Loons also become mottled and drab when they winter in the warm climates of the south. Only when spring returns and the Loons fly to the northern lakes do they grow their striking plumage.

But perhaps the greatest difference between these birds is their voices. The Grebe's *kuk-kuk-kuk* sound is dull compared to the Loon's cry. As twilight falls on the northern wilderness, the haunting calls of the Northern Diver echo across the calm, open water. The Loon has many voices: a laughlike tremolo (really a call of concern), a yodel, a hoot, and an eerie wolflike wail. For many listeners no other birdcall can equal the mystical cries of the Loon.

Epilogue

Water birds are intricately connected to their environment. When it is stable, they flourish, but when it is unbalanced, they are threatened. Diseases and predators can have disastrous effects on their numbers. Droughts reduce their food source and dry up the inland swamps that are nesting sites for many species. Floods can scatter fish and other aquatic life, forcing the older birds to abandon their young and fly greater distances in search of food.

Although water birds are resourceful, they need our attention to survive. Civilization may be their greatest threat. Encroachment upon the wetlands, and drainage of the birds' habitat can quickly reduce their population. Pollution and pesticides also threaten their survival. And so we observe them and learn, and in the process we discover the sense of wonder these birds and their special world can inspire. As long as the waterways last, there will be water birds.

Bibliography

Austin, Oliver L., Jr. *Birds of the World*. New York: Golden Press, 1961.

Bradbury, Will. *Birds of Sea, Shore, and Stream*. The Wild, Wild World of Animals Series. New York: A Time/Life Television Book produced in association with Vineyard Books, Inc., 1976.

Brooks, Bruce. *On the Wing*. New York: Charles Scribner's Sons, 1989.

Brown, Joseph E. *The Return of the Brown Pelican*. Baton Rouge: Louisiana State University Press, 1983.

Carr, Archie, and the editors of Time/Life Books. *The Everglades*. The American Wilderness Series. New York: Time/Life Books, 1973.

de Golia, Jack. *Everglades: The Story behind the Scenery*. Las Vegas: KC Publications, 1978.

Eckert, Allan W. *The Wading Birds of North America (North of Mexico)*. Garden City, N.Y.: Doubleday and Co., Inc., 1981.

Gallagher, Tim. "The Great Blue Heron." *Wildbird Magazine*. July 1989, p. 13.

Hancock, James, and James Kushlan. *The Heron's Handbook*. New York: Harper and Row, 1984.

Line, Les, Kimball L. Garrett, and Ken Kaufman. *The Audubon Society Book of Water Birds*. New York: Harry N. Abrams, Inc., 1987.

McIlhenny, E. A. *Autobiography of an Egret*. New York: Hastings House, 1939.

Ogden, John C. "The Abundant Endangered Flinthead." *Audubon Magazine*. January 1983, p. 90.

Palmer, Ralph, ed. *Handbook of North American Birds*. Volumes 2 and 3. New Haven: Yale University Press, 1973.

Peterson, Roger Tory. *The Birds*. New York: Time/Life Books, 1968.

Russell, Franklin. *Wings on the Southwind: Birds and Creatures of Southern Wetlands*. Birmingham, Ala.: Oxmoor House, 1984.

Scott, Jack Denton. *That Wonderful Pelican*. New York: G. P. Putnam's Sons, 1983.

Terres, John K. *The Audubon Society Encyclopedia of North American Birds*. New York: Alfred A. Knopf, 1980.

Wetmore, Alexander. *Water, Prey, and Game Birds of North America*. Washington, D.C.: National Geographic Society, 1965.

Williams, Winston. *Florida's Fabulous Waterbirds—Their Stories*. n.p.: World-Wide Printing, 1987.

Index